Oddly Distracted

A
Ger
cartoon collection

Edited by Gerard Whyman

All cartoons copyright of Gerard Whyman 2008

The right of Gerard Whyman to be identified as author of this work has been asserted by him in accordance with the Copyright, Designs and Patent Act, 1988.

ISBN 978 0 9559793 0 9

Published by Gerard Whyman 2008

Design and layout by Gerard Whyman

www.gerardwhyman.co.uk

All rights reserved. No part of this publication may be reproduced or transmitted in any form or means, electronic or mechanical including photocopying, recording or any information storage or retrieval system without prior permission in writing from the publisher.

*To my mum and my dad,
who liked a laugh.*

"What sort of work are you looking for?"

'Oddly Distracted'. A strange title, perhaps. Well, if these cartoons appear to be the product of a slightly distracted mind I can live with that. I couldn't possibly comment on the 'odd' bit, however.

I didn't set out to be a cartoonist. My childhood ambition was to be a car designer. Given the moribund state of the British car industry I'd say my eventual career path as a cartoonist wasn't such a bad choice. There's a 'car' in the word at least. I figured that most British car designers were closet cartoonists anyway. How else would you explain the Austin Allegro?

This is a fairly representative selection of work produced over the last dozen years or so. Representative in as much as many of them have been rejected by one editor or another. Not rejected by me I hasten to add. Some of my favourite gags are seeing print for the first time in this collection.

Hopefully it's largely cliche free though if one or two 'shrink' or dalek jokes have slipped through the net I'm afraid that's par for the course in cartoon land. There are, I admit, a large number of religious jokes here too. That may be a legacy of my Catholic upbringing but more likely to be a result of my love of the Dave Allen show in the 1970's.

Anyway, please enjoy this book. I hope you'll be happily distracted by it for a long time to come!

All the best,

Gerard Whyman, July 2008

"I chose the decor and my wife chose the furniture."

"You've gone too far with that handlebar moustache!"

"Really, Derek, must you make a big scene out of everything?"

"Bloody hell, not more hippy hikers!"

"Your grandfather doesn't say much these days.
All he does is just look into space."

"I'm sorry, Mr Tindall, your face doesn't quite fit."

"There's no room in this company for sentiment so I'm going to have to let you go, Little Timkins."

"Don't worry, sir - you'll soon bounce back."

"But it's only got one star!"

"Go on, admit it, you got that gold from Argos, didn't you?"

"I heard Jesus saves so I invested the gold!"

"Sorry, Denise - mother hasn't taken to you."

"Yeah, the cat's pretty territorial."

GUIDE DOG FOR THE BLAND

"The doctor hasn't much time for us these days."

"I'm a bit concerned about your high cholesterol level, Mr Dumpty."

"I wanted a bigger congregation so I asked God for a sign."

"Sorry, sir, all our bitter's are off."

"Thank you for your thoughts on our product placement, Mr Chico."

"What he needs is a good PR person!"

"You haven't got what I'm not looking for."

"It's the only way I can get people in on a Sunday."

"I'm a bit worried about Tim's lack of progress."

"It must be a youth culture!"

"Can we have someone other than Jenkins this time?"

"*Right, let's start with the basics!*"

"I think the new boy lied on his application form."

"It's not my idea of a stretch limo!"

"It's about all these insurance claims you've been making..."

"HOUSE!"

"Those bendy buses are beginning to have an affect on the passengers."

"Have you thought of claiming a severance payment?"

"Oh no, he's turned into Long John Silver Surfer!"

"...and I did these drawings for the kid's room!"

"I hate him, he's so two faced."

"Silly cow forgot to put her landing lights on."

"Oh, wow! You got high definition!"

"I hate these trailers before the main event."

"That's the last time we have curried herring."

"Michael can do wonderful things with pasta."

"He's ever so good with children!"

"Nonsense! What makes you think you'll be under her thumb?"

"It's his 'trophy wife' - unfortunately he came third."

"Admiring my trophy cabinet I see, Hodges."

"You can't 'read me like a book', Darren - you're illiterate!"

"You lucky devil, most people just find some loose change under the cushions."

"I must say, I'm shocked by your latest fashion statement!"

"Studio creche? This is the scriptwriters' office!"

"Right then, Davey, Suzi, Little Johnny, Fran, Simon and Pretty Polly. Are we all sitting comfortably? Good, then I'll begin..."

"...and Ruth, how have long working hours affected your lifestyle?"

"I'd like a word about the length of your breaks, Jenkins!"

"New installation? I suppose so, I'm putting in the new gas boiler."

"I prefer his earlier work."

"...and this one is from the school of 'What's the Pointilism'."

"I thought we'd try some regression therapy this week, Mr Smith."

"My neighbour has a bit of a drink problem."

"It's against building regulations."

"We specialize in designing tower blocks."

"Play down the damp problem with that one, Jenkins."

"...that gingerbread should be 1 foot thick, marshmallow isn't an adequate insulation material..."

SORCERER'S APPRENTICE

"Of course he looks superior - he's our new line manager."

"Look, we sell insurance so cut out all the 'meaning of life' stuff!"

"Oh God, here comes Mr Mid-Life Crisis!"

The Royal Wii

"I take it you're having a quiet retirement."

"It's the Avon Lady of the Lake calling."

"In this one Jesus marries a hat stand."

"You can tell the artist really loves this medium."

"I do a lot of dental work for celebrities."

"A simple bottle would have sufficed for your sample."

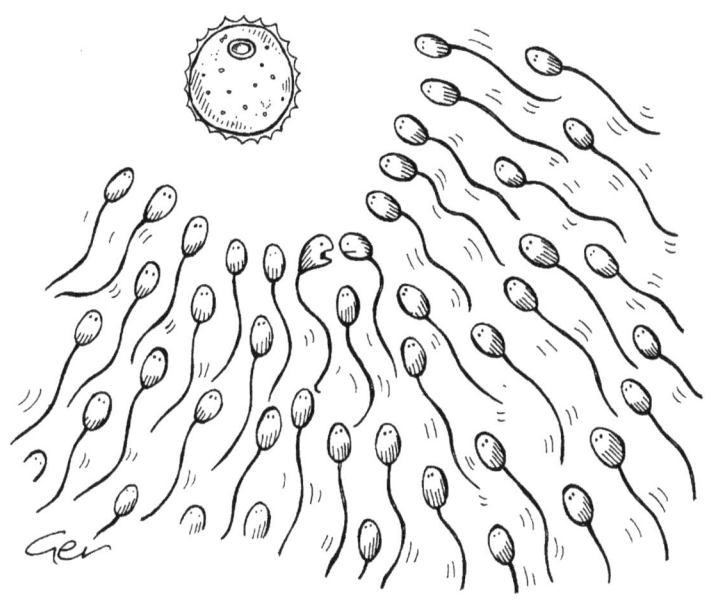

"Looks like egg for breakfast!"

The cloning experiment was disappointing - you could say I'm not quite beside myself."

"It's payback time, Johnny - now enter your PIN!"

"Oh no, it's the Mafioso Kid!"

"Leave it, Keith, he looks a bit handy!"

"Nonsense, lad, what makes you think I'm going to sell you?"

"Our passing has been really slick this year."

"Bless me Father for I have been sin binned."

"It's the parents' 4 x 4 x 400 metres!"

"Darren, haven't you bought your homework off the Internet yet?"

"Can you do eyes, a mouth, a nose - that sort of thing?"

"We've been playing tag, mum."

"Ken's under a lot of pressure at work."

"It's more than just a spider in the bath, love!"

"No wonder you have trouble communicating - the cartoonist didn't give you mouths."

"I fancied a smoothie for breakfast."

PHISHERMAN'S FRIEND

"*This is hell, my friend - of course we still use MS-DOS.*"

"We've updated it - it's now a Wickerpaedia Man!"

"Be honest, doctor, how bad is it?"

"You're not getting any of it - it's all going to a cats' home!"

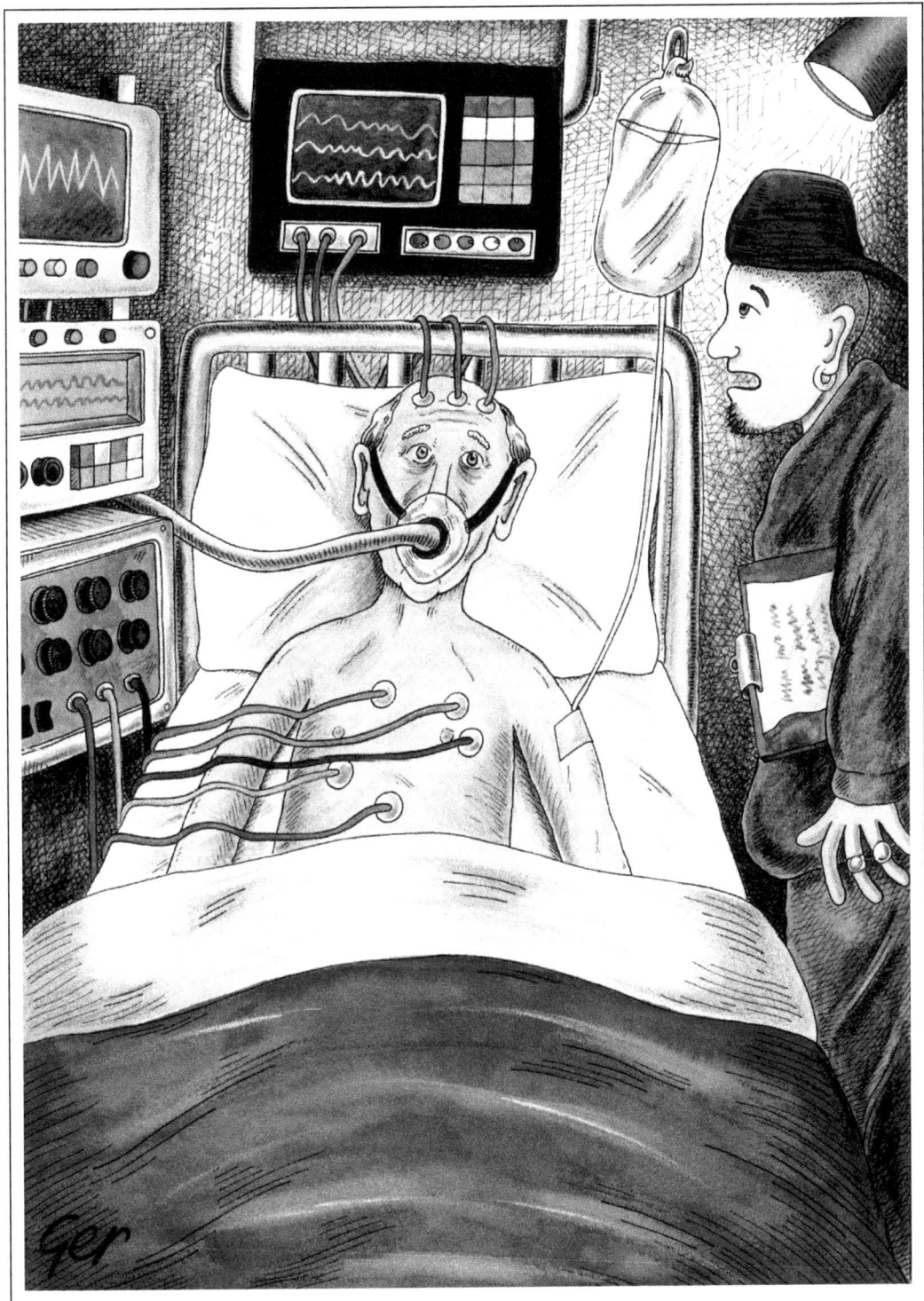

"Hi, I'm Andy from hospital radio - any last requests?"

"Good grief, what sort of 'sniffer' dog is that?"

"Wow, that's some guide dog!"

"Huh, don't tell me she hasn't had plastic surgery."

"Not another scratch card!"

"Well, it's not my idea of breakfast in bed!"

"So, it's really over then, Jill?"

"No, I'm not having a 'relaxing, candlelit' bath - the boiler's on the blink again!"

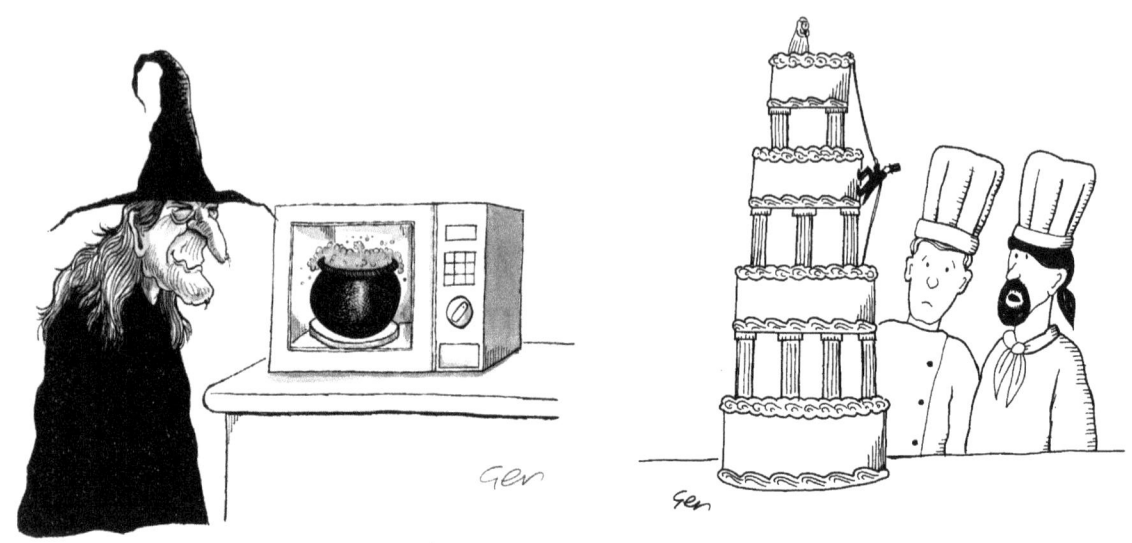

"The bridegroom is a mountaineer apparently."

"Nobody does curses like Gordon Ramsay."

FORSYTE'S AGAS

"What, Master Oliver, you want LESS?!"

"Well, at least the education system is working."

"Look, I don't like 'bring your child to work' day any more than you do."

"Right, who threw that?"

"Great Lotus position, Tabitha."

"I parked the limo around the corner, sir."

"Can I bring Jesus into your life, madam?"

"Why can't we just pretend to be out when the double glazing salesman calls?"

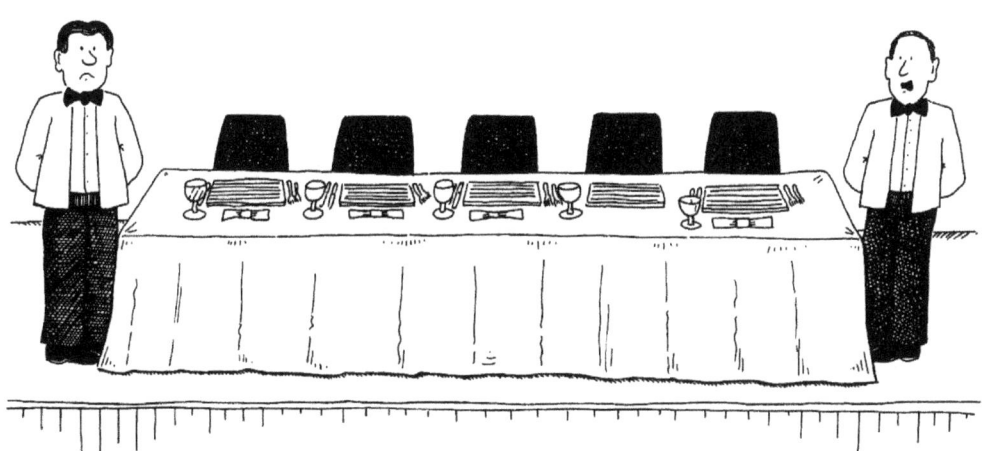
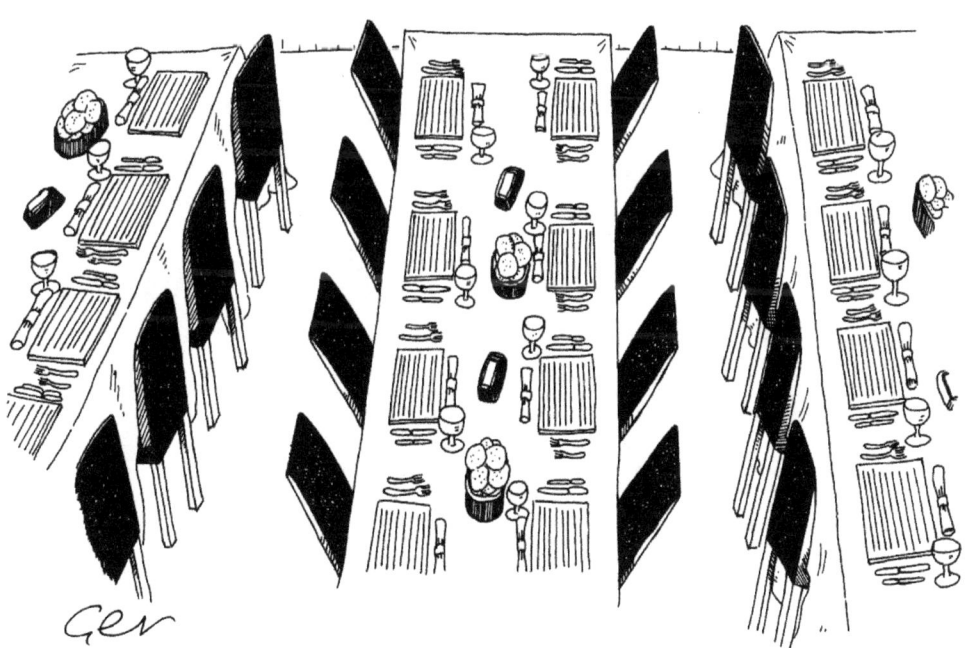

"It's the same thing every year - they never let any of them in."

"Can't you see I've got a fair in the back already?"

"I dunno - it looks a bit dodgy to me."

"I think spring is on the way!"

"I've invested in my future."

"Bless you!"

"Does this mean this week's WI meeting is off, Mabel?"

"You're quite proud of your reputation as an office bully, aren't you?

"Mark my words, son, you're going to be massive!"

POWER BREAKFAST

"Judging from your C.V. you're a very confident person."

"Do you have an appointment?"

"You must heal yourself!"

"Does my bum look big enough in this?"

"You've got the wrong idea about 'going Dutch'!"

"Oh darling, it's the best present ever!"

"Ken's a lovely man - in fact, he's all heart!"

"I'm a man of substance - most of them illegal!"

"I wish they'd make the drugs tests more dignified."

"Looks like another split bag, Eric!"

"Honestly, madam, every home should have one."

"I converted the loft."

"We want it painted the colour of money."

"OI!"

"This is a room with a 'deja view'!"

"I told you this place has gone downhill."

"*Bloody falsies!*"

"He was a randy devil apparently."

"My God, Cuthbert, it's an E-Type Jag!"

"It's not what I had in mind for Big Game hunting!"

"Looks like 'Son of Big Foot'!"

"The kids wanted to move into something more up to date."

"Not much of a miracle if you ask me - it's been turned into Blue Nun."

"Of course, it would be more impressive if the tide was in."

"Oh, I was expecting 3 Kings!"

The cartoons with page numbers were originally published in:

Independent on Sunday magazine - *page 4 and 16 bottom*
Punch - *pages 7, 9 bottom, 10 top, 24 bottom, 25, 37 top, 38 bottom, 42 top & bottom, 43 bottom, 44 top, 53 top, 58 top, 63 bottom, 72 bottom, 73, 75 bottom, 76 top, 87, 98 bottom, 99 and 104 top left*
The Phoenix - *pages 17 bottom, 19, 27, 28 top & bottom, 60 top left, 70 top & bottom, 80 top, 94 top & 108 bottom*
The Oldie - *pages 8 top, 16 top, 41, 78 top right, 84 bottom and 107 bottom and 111*
The Spectator - *pages 8 bottom, 12 top, 15, 22 bottom, 28 bottom, 32 bottom, 33 top, 37 bottom, 38 top, 45 bottom, 46 top left & right, 49 top, 51, 52 top, 62 top, 74 bottom and 75 top*
The New Statesman - *page 43 top*
Maxim - *pages 9 top, 14 bottom and 28 top*
The Times Metro supplement - *page 50 bottom*
Private Eye - *pages 39 bottom, 79 top*
Reader's Digest - *pages 38 bottom, 56 top & bottom, 58 bottom, 60 bottom, 62 top, 65, 66 top & bottom, 71, 94 bottom and 97 top*
Prospect - *page 68 top*
Fiesta - *page 104 bottom*

Many of the other cartoons have been published in a variety of trade magazines, journals, 'in house' publications, exhibition catalogues and calendars.

Thanks to Steve Way,
Richard Curtis (no, not that one)
& Royston Robertson

www.gerardwhyman.co.uk

"Meaning of Life? Next floor up, son!"

www.ingramcontent.com/pod-product-compliance
Ingram Content Group UK Ltd.
Pitfield, Milton Keynes, MK11 3LW, UK
UKHW051254180426
11947UKWH00020B/1712